AF593825

MALCOLM'S CHOICE

1. *F.R. Finch*

'The drill is to deliver a mildly blasphemous address, get Fleet Street to call you a turbulent priest, and you're in the big time.'

MALCOLM'S CHOICE

1. *F.R. Finch*

'The drill is to deliver a mildly blasphemous address, get Fleet Street to call you a turbulent priest, and you're in the big time.'

Malcolm's Choice

A COLLECTION OF CARTOONS

Compiled and Introduced by

MALCOLM MUGGERIDGE

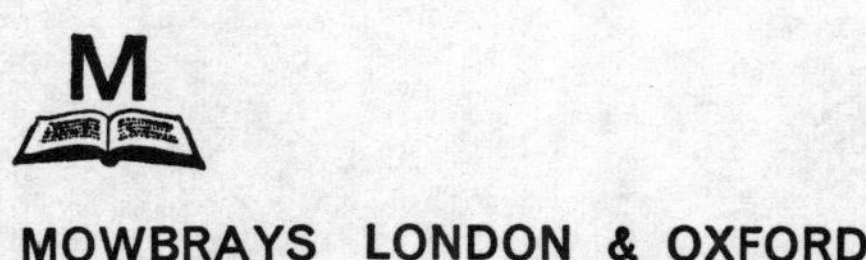

MOWBRAYS LONDON & OXFORD

FOREWORD

When I was editor of *Punch* I used to brood intermittently and sadly on how humour seemed to be in very short supply. The reason, I decided, was that the religion of materialism, the most widely practised today, has by its nature to be completely serious. Once the claims advertisers make for their products are exposed to ridicule, there is the danger that the whole mystique of salesmanship will be brought into disrepute, and the consumer society with it. An extreme example of what I mean is provided by a happening I heard about in a Marseilles brothel. It seems that a blue film being shown there caused one of the clients watching it to start laughing uproariously. He was at once thrown out on the ground that his laughter counteracted the film's desired effect in drumming up business.

Following the same line of thought, it seemed to me clear that the supply of clerical humour varies in direct ratio with the available supply of religious faith. Rabelais flourished in a great age of faith, St Francis was always laughing, but how is it possible to make a joke about Dr John Robinson, Karl Barth or Lord Soper? To circumvent this difficulty, we used on *Punch* to pretend that people still went to church, vicars were still liable to be shocked and missionaries to be eaten, that bishops continued to press the tips of their fingers together and to be bullied by their wives, and curates to make fatuous observations and to be pursued by any ladies in their congregations with matrimonial aspirations. In other words, we just assumed that Barchester was still going strong, comforting ourselves with the thought that Osbert Lancaster, the acknowledged maestro in the *genre*, did likewise, in the sense that he located his clerics—the famous Fontwater, for instance—rather in the Athenaeum Club than in country or town rectories, their native habitat.

Such a device could not be continued for ever, and I note in the cartoons collected here a serious effort to extract humour from contemporary clerical figures like the trendy clergyman. For instance: 'The drill is to deliver a mildly blasphemous address, get Fleet Street to call you a turbulent priest, and you're in the big time.' My only comment is: Why 'mildly'? There is, I should say, a good deal more mileage to be got out of this particular theme. At Evensong recently, in a country church, I heard a moon-faced curate with lavish mutton-chop whiskers pray that we all might be made 'thinkers like Karl Marx', adding, presumably lest there should be any misunderstanding on high, 'some of whose ideas are good and some bad'. Looking round at the congregation I doubted whether any very strong aspiration to be thinkers like Karl Marx existed among them, and wondered what Marx himself, wherever he happens now to be, would make of so droll an orison if it came his way.

There are always, of course, the religious orders, which are supposed to be less subject to change than secular religious institutions. Jokes about haloes, I am glad to see, continue to appear regularly, and nuns go on presenting certain comic artists with an irresistible attraction. Even this field, however, may be jeopardized if present trends continue, whereby, especially in America, nuns use make-up, wear mini-skirts and generally comport themselves like air-hostesses. Nonetheless, we may comfort ourselves with the thought that as long as Man continues to be religious—which he always must, or cease to be Man—jokes about his transcendental aspirations will continue to be produced. It was not by chance that the builders of the Mediaeval cathedrals put gargoyles as well as steeples on them. Humour, I decided after five gruelling years in the business, may be defined as an expression in terms of the grotesque of the enormous disparity between human aspirations and human performance. On this basis, our everlasting quest for God, besides taking us to the most sublime heights, will likewise continue to dissolve us from time to time in equally sublime laughter.

MALCOLM MUGGERIDGE

INDEX to ARTISTS

ACKNOWLEDGEMENTS

The Publishers wish to thank all the artists who submitted cartoons, and to congratulate those whose work was selected.

The publishers also gratefully acknowledge those who have given permission for the reproduction of the following cartoons: Nos. 5, 11, 16, 20, 35, 40, 44, 48, 50, 51, 75, 89 which first appeared in *Punch*; No. 7, 32 which first appeared in *Focus*; No. 1, 72 which first appeared in *Crusade*; No. 37, 81 which first appeared in *Worship and Preaching*; No. 42 which first appeared in *The Sign*. Apology is made to anyone whose cartoon has unwittingly been reproduced without permission.

The photograph on page four is by Max Ehlert.

Printed in Great Britain by Alden & Mowbray Ltd at the Alden Press, Oxford

ISBN 0 264 64599 5

First published 1972

A. R. Mowbray & Co Ltd, The Alden Press, Osney Mead, Oxford, OX2 OEG

2. *Field*

'Do get a move on, Tubby, it's full drag tonight, you know.'

3. *G.G. Walker*

'Well, have I passed?'

4. *Colin Earl*

'Here endeth the first lesson!'

5. ***Leslie Starke***

'Before I remove my shirt, Doctor, I'd like to explain that I was ordained late in life.'

6. ***Paul Champkins***

'The Vicar is out exorcising the dog.'

7. *Richard Grasby*

'Very well, Mr. Dean — just as you say, but I hope we're not going to have this Common Market touch on the hymn board every Sunday.'

8. *Palios*

9. *Bartlam*

'Well — be good!'

10. *A.F. Ralley*

'Just like my missus, she hasn't even had it put in the obituary column.'

11.

Leslie Starke

'You'll have to excuse the mess — we've got the decorator in.'

12. *T. Bayley Hughes*

13. *D. Baker*

'I thought we could have a collection for the Vicar's birthday, but I put all my buttons in the offertory.'

14. *Bill Bowden*

15. *Bartlam*

'Well, well – talk of the devil . . .!'

16. *Leslie Starke*

'What can one do, dear? – except perhaps roll up the window.'

17. *V.E. Cox/R. Poulter*

'Here they come again – angels from the realms of Crawley.'

18. *David Downe*

'I'll take any Soul-destroying job.'

19. *James D. Crocker*

20. *F.R. Finch*

'I don't like his "Unholier than thou" attitude.'

21. *Gordon Stowell*

'Good morning Mr. Jones! and welcome to our informal Sunday morning service for Sportsmen!'

22. *D. Grey*

'At times I'm tempted to pray, Almighty and most Perciful God. Mrs. Simpkins.'

23. *Bartlam*

'Ten seconds to go, Reverend, – now give them all you've got!'

24. *Field*

'And now, in honour of our theatrical friends who are with us today let us all join in that glorious final number from their smash-hit "Hair" . . .'

25. *Field*

'Doesn't miss a trick. He's visiting the Holy Land for a TV series – "In the Footsteps of Malcolm Muggeridge".'

26. ***D. Baker***

'You realise that if our No-work-on-the-Sabbath campaign is a success, we shall be out of work ourselves.'

27. ***A.C. Phillips***

'No dear, I don't expect the Vicar gets double time on Sunday like Daddy!'

28. ***T. Bayley Hughes***

29. ***Palios***

'You know, Brainswait, perhaps your motto "Heels re-souled" is going to work.'

30. *Barry Knowles*

'Are you *sure* we're not building this thing too high, Bert?'

31. *Bill Bowden*

'Sorry I overslept – I forgot to feed my alarm last night.'

32. *Richard Grasby*

'. . . and see to it that the steeple leans by one cloth yard, then as soon as this church is finished we can start the restoration fund.'

33. *Gordon Stowell*

'Confound these choirboys and their wretched science experiments!'

34. *J.B. Lawry*

'It'll be your word against mine!'

35. *Leslie Starke*

'Well, don't just stand there – turn him over and loosen his collar!'

36. *T. Bayley Hughes*

'If the old version was good enough for St. Paul it's good enough for me.!'

37. ***F.R. Finch***

'I don't much care for this "more-charismatic-than-thou" attitude.'

38. *G.G. Walker*

'He had no right to come here if he couldn't stand heights.'

39. ***Bartlam***

'He was a big noise in the television world!'

Leslie Starke

41. *Paul Champkins*

'Brother James is our bell ringer.'

42. ***Bill Bowden***

'For the purposes of instruction we'll call this one Ding and that one Dong.'

43. *Vernon Sundfors*

'This is your sky-pilot speaking . . .'

44. *Leslie Starke*

'Just a minute Charlie, let's have another look at that delivery docket.'

45. *Bartlam*

'And why did the Vicar say – turned out nice again – to you!'

46. *T. Bayley Hughes*

' – and to obey.'

47. *A.C. Phillips*

'Mum says your son is a proper little devil!'

48. *Leslie Starke*

'It's the way he put it, Ethel. He asked if he could stay up for the Epilogue.'

49. *R.W. Genney*

'The organ will have to go for a start.'

50. *Leslie Starke*

'I'm absolutely famished. Couldn't we save time by saying Grace now!'

51. *Leslie Starke*

'Nice shot, Vicar!'

52. *Bartlam*

'At least they will have a taste of religion!'

53. *Colin Earl*

'. . . and for all those that watch television, let's put it another way — there are two kinds of people, goodies and baddies.'

54. *Bill Bowden*

'Beware brother – skinheads!'

55. *James D. Crocker*

56. *Colin Earl*

'I haven't seen you for the last few Sundays — I trust you haven't been bad.'

57; *Field*

'Snap!'

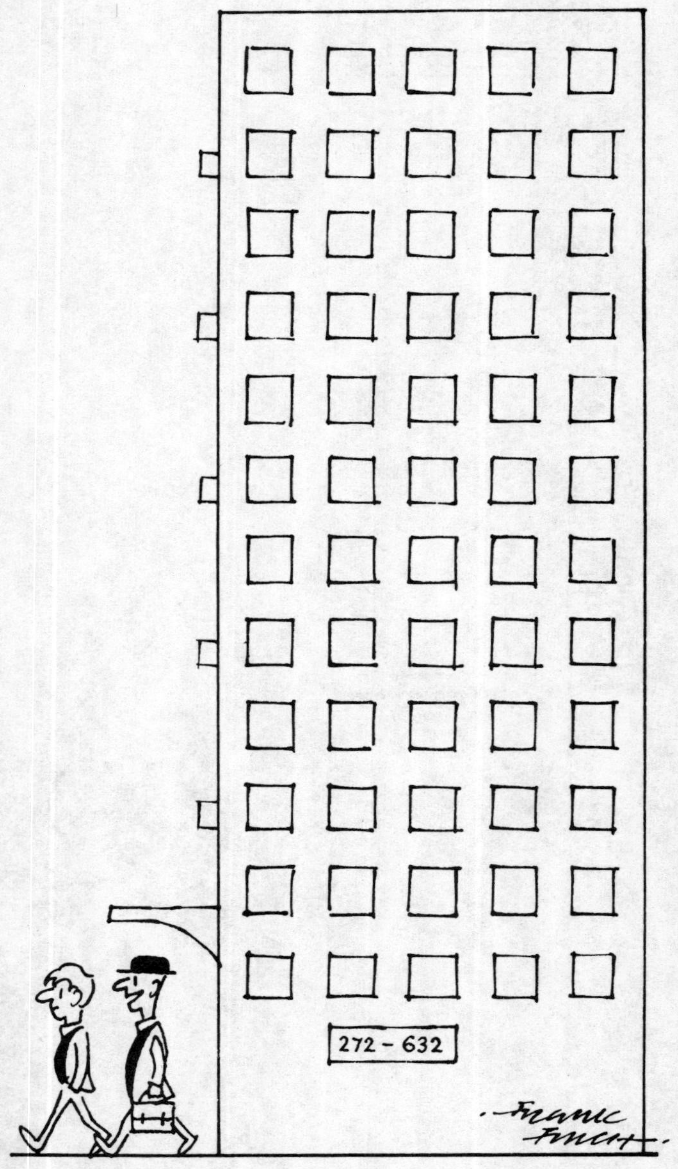

58. ***F.R. Finch***

'See what I mean, Pickering? – nothing like getting to know your congregation at the grass roots.'

59. *Bartlam*

'He hasn't quite the hang of bell ringing!'

60. *A.F. Ralley*

'Maybe the good Lord will look after you when you go, but He won't look after your missus.'

61. *A.M. Shanks*

'The tradesman's entrance is round the back.'

62. *James D. Crocker*

'Act nonchalant!'

63. *G.G. Walker*

'He's giving him hell!'

64. *A.C. Phillips*

'I can't help what the fashion is outside Sister Kelly – we can't have mini-skirts in here!'

65. *T. Bayley Hughes*

'You'd better call on Mrs. Hawkins number 26 – she hasn't been at the whist drive for a fortnight.'

66. *A.F. Ralley*

'I made you an angel cake dear.'

67. *Capon*

68. *Colin Earl*

69. *Marguerite Mills*

'Why did you not come to church? I said you were to practise abstinence in Lent, not absence.'

70. *T. Bayley Hughes*

'Keep taking the tablets Vicar and we'll have you on your knees in no time!'

71. ***Bill Bowden***

72. ***F.R. Finch***

'And another thing Edgar – continuing dialogue could mean a long succession of lovely conferences like this.'

73. ***Gordon Stowell***

74. *A.M. Shanks*

'I don't give a damn what St. Patrick says, you're not coming in here with that parcel!'

75. ***Leslie Starke***

76. *Peter A. Clarke*

'What's it to you what I do on my day off!'

77. ***Bartlam***

'Relax Herbert – it's *Monday* morning!'

78. ***Mrs. S. C. Walsh***

'But you *said* we were having the Archdeacon for dinner!'

79. *T. Bayley Hughes*

80. *G.G. Walker*

'. . . but keep it under your hat!'

81. ***F.R. Finch***

'We thought, Sir, that a poster like this might pull them in.'

82. ***J.C. Armitage***

'Have you read any good banns recently.'

83.

F.C. Bishop

'Aah! Walkies.'

84.

T. Bayley Hughes

85. *G.G. Walker*

'That's the hot line.'

86. *Bartlam*

'No hair cream thank you – just sprinkle a few ashes on!'

87. *Peter A. Clarke*

'. . . and under the Trades Description Act . . .'

88. *Bill Bowden*

89. *Leslie Starke*

'As I was parking outside I made a big dent in a big blue Riley saloon.'

90. *T. Bayley Hughes*

91. *Bartlam*

'What's this I hear about you three appearing on television!'

92. *J.B. Lawry*

'You'll have to go on a diet.'

93. *Bartlam*

'Yah — skinhead.'

94. *A.C. Phillips*

'I hear there was a good Tarzan film on telly last night Brother Simpkin!'

95. *Bartlam*

'Really Fotheringay – not in front of your father!'

96. ***David Downe***

'You are kind, charitable, considerate, you don't covet another man's ox nor his ass.'

97. ***Bill Bowden***

'A slow dignified paddling motion will suffice, Brother Krushnic.'

98. *G.G. Walker*

'The sexton happens to be an optician, Ma'am.'

99. *D. Grey*

100. *Colin Earl*